JN062917

Revised Edition

PRACTICAL SITUATIONS FOR THE TOEIC® TEST LISTENING

Kayo Yoshida Kyoko Nakanishi Shizuka Itagaki Brian Covert

改訂新版

実生活で役立つTOEIC®テストリスニング

音声ファイルのダウンロード／ストリーミング

CD マーク表示がある箇所は、音声を弊社 HP より無料でダウンロード／ストリーミングすることができます。トップページのバナーをクリックし、書籍検索してください。書籍詳細ページに音声ダウンロードアイコンがございますのでそちらから自習用音声としてご活用ください。

https://www.seibido.co.jp

PRACTICAL SITUATIONS FOR THE TOEIC® TEST LISTENING
Revised Edition

はじめに

　本書は、2016年5月に改定された新形式のTOEIC®（Test of English for International Communication）に対応したListening Part対策教材です。主に500点以上のスコアを目指す学習者を対象に作成していますが、これからTOEIC®を受験しようという人、また、リスニング力を継続的に伸ばしていきたいという人にも利用していただける教材です。

　各章10問のMiniテスト形式の問題を通して、試験形式や出題傾向に慣れ、頻出単語を習得し、着実にリスニング力を養っていくことを目的としています。新形式に導入された3人による会話、図表を伴う問題、語彙が暗示する意味を問う設問もバランスよく、効果的に学習できるようになっています。全部で20章立てとなっており、さらに4回分のReviewテストもついています。

　実社会で役立つ英語力も同時に身につくよう、テキストの内容は海外生活における習慣や行事、季節に関するテーマで構成されており、日常生活の様々な場面で適切な対応ができるように工夫がなされています。

　授業の最初の小テストとして、また、リスニングの力を定期的にチェックする副教材として活用することで、効果的に授業が組み立てられ、話題の導入もスムーズに行うことが可能です。

　短時間でも継続的に学習することでリスニングの力がつき、最終的にTOEIC®のListening Partのスコアを飛躍的に伸ばすことが可能です。

　本書が、今後TOEIC®を受験する学習者の役に立ち、また、実用的な英語力の向上につながることを願ってやみません。

　最後に、本書の刊行にあたり、様々なご提案をいただき、私たち著者からの無理な要望にも丁寧に対応して下さった成美堂編集部の皆様に心より感謝を申し上げます。

2019年9月　著者一同

本書の構成と利用法

■ Point

TOEIC®によく出題され、また、日常生活でも役立つ表現やボキャブラリーを各Unitのテーマに沿って取り上げています。Pointで学習した語彙の大半は、その後に続くWarm-upやPart 1 〜 Part 4の問題に含まれており、段階的かつ効率的に語彙を習得できるようにまとめています。

■ Warm-up Exercise

リスニングによる空所補充問題です。Pointで学習した表現や語句を聴くことで発音やアクセント、イントネーション等を確認し、書き取ることでより記憶に残るように工夫しています。後に続くリスニング問題をスムーズに理解するWarm-upの役割をし、TOEIC®の試験でもよく使われる重要表現を厳選しています。

■ Mini-TOEIC®: Part 1 〜 4

Listening PartのPart 1からPart 4までを10問にまとめたMini-TOEIC®形式で、短時間で問題形式や出題傾向がつかめる構成になっています。新形式に導入された3人による会話、図表を伴う問題、語彙が暗示する意味を問う設問も、効果的に学習できるようになっており、アメリカ英語だけでなく、カナダ・イギリス・オーストラリアの英語で発音された問題をバランスよく混ぜています。

■ Review Test 1 〜 4

テキストの最後に4つの復習テストがついています。Review Test 1はUnit 1 〜 5、Review Test 2はUnit 6 〜 10、Review Test 3はUnit 11 〜 15、Review Test 4はUnit 16 〜 20で学習したボキャブラリーや日常表現が復習できるようになっており、それぞれ15問のMini-TOEIC®形式で構成されています。各学期の中間や期末の時期に、リスニング能力や語彙力の確認のために利用されることをお勧めします。

■ Mini-TOEIC®の問題数と構成

Unit 1 〜 20 （各10問）

Part 1 (写真描写問題：Photographs) ---2問
Part 2 (応答問題：Question & Response) --- 4問
Part 3 (会話問題：Short Conversations) --- 2問 〔1題〕
Part 4 (説明文問題：Short Talks) --- 2問 〔1題〕

Review Test 1 〜 4 （各15問）

Part 1 (写真描写問題：Photographs) ---4問
Part 2 (応答問題：Question & Response) --- 5問
Part 3 (会話問題：Short Conversations) --- 3問 〔1題〕
Part 4 (説明文問題：Short Talks) --- 3問 〔1題〕

Contents

Unit 1 Ceremony
~It's a pleasure to meet you.~

☑ Point: 挨拶に関する表現

ご機嫌を伺う表現	返答例
How are you? / How are you doing? What's new? / How have you been? Is everything all right?	Very well, thanks. How about you? Not (too) bad. / Same as always. Pretty good, thank you. And you?
自己紹介の表現	返答例
Hello. My name is ～. Please call me ～. I'd like to introduce myself. I'm ～. Let me introduce myself. My name is ～.	(It's) Nice to meet you. I'm ～. (I'm) Pleased to meet you. It's a pleasure to meet you.
別れ際の挨拶	
Nice meeting you. It was good to see you again. I hope to see you again very soon.	It was nice talking with you. Take care. Let's keep in touch. See you then. / See you again. / See you later.

📝 Warm-up Exercise: Greetings 1-02

1. Good morning. Welcome to my class. It's a (   ) to meet you all.

2. May I (   ) your name, please? ----- Sure. My name is Thomas Brown.
   Just (   ) me Tom.

3. How are you (   )? ----- I'm all right, and you?

4. I'd like to introduce (   ). I'm Sandra River.
   ----- Hello, Ms. River. Thanks for coming.

5. Hi, I'm Mark Smith from ABC Company.
   ----- (   ) to meet you. Please have a seat.

🔊 Mini-TOEIC® Listening

| Part 1 | Photographs | 1-03, 04 |

1.

(A) (B) (C) (D)

2.

(A) (B) (C) (D)

Part 2   Question-Response

3. Mark your answer on your answer sheet.   (A) (B) (C)

4. Mark your answer on your answer sheet.   (A) (B) (C)

5. Mark your answer on your answer sheet.   (A) (B) (C)

6. Mark your answer on your answer sheet.   (A) (B) (C)

Part 3   Short Conversation

7. What can be inferred from this conversation?

(A) Ken is an international student.

(B) Mako is Ken's conversation partner.

(C) Mako's friend came from Japan.

(D) Ken is a first-year university student.

8. Look at the map. Which dormitory does Ken probably live in?

(A) Queen's Court
(B) Mansfield Hall
(C) Exeter House
(D) Spencer Court

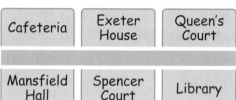

Cafeteria	Exeter House	Queen's Court
Mansfield Hall	Spencer Court	Library

Part 4   Short Talk

9. Which institution is Dr. Brown working for?

(A) Cambridge University

(B) Bristol University

(C) Brisbane University

(D) London University

10. When was Dr. Brown awarded his degree?

(A) In 2000

(B) In 1997

(C) In 1977

(D) In 1973

(1 点×10)

Class	No.	Name	Score	/10

2

Unit 2 School Life
~What do you major in?~

☑ Point: 自己紹介に関する表現

- freshman「(大学)1年」 ● sophomore「2年生」 ● junior「3年」 ● senior「4年」
- major「専攻(する)」 ● department「学部、学科」 ● dormitory (dorm)「学生寮」
- register「登録する」 ● sign up「申し込む」 ● assignment「課題、宿題」
- credit / unit「単位」 ● bachelor's degree「学士号」 ● master's degree「修士号」
- doctor's degree (Ph.D)「博士号」
- (post-) graduate student「大学院生」 ● undergraduate student「学部生」
- semester「学期(前期、後期の 場合)」 ● term「学期」

📝 Warm-up Exercise: Introducing yourself 1-13

1. What do you (   )? ----- I'm a (   ) student at Kent University.

2. What is your major? ----- I (   ) (   ) computer science.

3. You need to (   ) for the courses you would like to take.
   ----- Where should I go?

4. Are you going to (   ) the orientation for freshmen? If so, you need to
   (   ) up soon.

5. To apply for a room in the university (   ), please (   ) out
   this form.

🧠 Mini-TOEIC® Listening

| Part 1 | Photographs | 1-14, 15

1.

(A) (B) (C) (D)

2.

(A) (B) (C) (D)

Part 2   Question-Response

 1-16~19

3. Mark your answer on your answer sheet.　　　(A) (B) (C)
4. Mark your answer on your answer sheet.　　　(A) (B) (C)
5. Mark your answer on your answer sheet.　　　(A) (B) (C)
6. Mark your answer on your answer sheet.　　　(A) (B) (C)

Part 3   Short Conversation

1-20, 21

7. What option has Judy been considering?
   (A) To major in two different subjects
   (B) To leave school
   (C) To move to a big city
   (D) To start a different area of study

8. When does Judy need to make a final decision on her major?
   (A) During the first year
   (B) During the second year
   (C) During the third year
   (D) During the final year

Part 4   Short Talk

1-22, 23

9. What does the man major in?
   (A) European studies
   (B) International studies
   (C) Cultural studies
   (D) Legal studies

10. Why is the university the man attends so attractive to him?
    (A) Because it accepts foreign students.
    (B) Because it gives an opportunity to study abroad.
    (C) Because it has a diverse teaching staff.
    (D) Because it has high academic standards.

(1 点×10)

Class	No.	Name	Score	/10

〈キリトリ線〉

Unit 3 Transportation
~How do you get to school?~

☑ Point: 交通機関に関する表現

- public transportation「公共交通機関」 ●traffic light「信号」 ●intersection「交差点」
- pedestrian crossing [crosswalk]「横断歩道」 ●passenger「乗客」
- express train「急行電車」 ●local train「各停電車」 ● (be) bound for「～行きの」
- one-way ticket「片道切符」 ●round-trip ticket「往復切符」 ●destination「目的地」
- arrival time「到着時間」 ●departure time「出発時間」 ●boarding pass「搭乗券」
- window seat「窓側席」 ●aisle seat「通路側席」 ●direct flight「直行便」
- connecting flight「乗り継ぎ便」 ●transit「乗り換え」 ●customs「税関」
- declaration「(税関での)申告」 ●quarantine「検疫所」
- baggage claim [reclaim]「手荷物受取所（引渡所）」

📝 Warm-up Exercise: Getting information

 1-24

1. Where is the nearest bus station? ----- It's next to the (   ) light.
2. Shall we take an express train to Green Station?
   ----- Only (   ) trains stop at that station.
3. Your train will be departing from Platform 3. But the (   ) time has been changed.
4. Would you prefer a window seat or an (   ) seat? ----- Either one is fine with me.
5. Passengers for North Airlines flight 777, (   ) for New York, will be (   ) from gate 5 within 20 minutes.

🧠 Mini-TOEIC® Listening

| Part 1 | Photographs | 1-25, 26 |

1.

(A) (B) (C) (D)

2.

(A) (B) (C) (D)

〈キリトリ線〉

Part 2 — Question-Response

 1-27~30

3. Mark your answer on your answer sheet. (A) (B) (C)
4. Mark your answer on your answer sheet. (A) (B) (C)
5. Mark your answer on your answer sheet. (A) (B) (C)
6. Mark your answer on your answer sheet. (A) (B) (C)

Part 3 — Short Conversation

1-31, 32

7. What does the man mean when he says, "I envy you!"?
   (A) He plans to travel and go sightseeing in London too.
   (B) He doesn't like business trips at all.
   (C) He is interested in the training program in the U.K.
   (D) He also wants to attend his high school reunion at a hotel.

8. What form of transportation will the woman mainly use when she is in London?
   (A) Bus
   (B) Train
   (C) Subway
   (D) Taxi

Part 4 — Short Talk

1-33, 34

9. What are the passengers advised to do?
   (A) Wait until the plane stops
   (B) Collect their personal belongings
   (C) Hold on to their bags tightly
   (D) Loosen their seat belts

10. If you have a temperature, what are you expected to do?
    (A) Go through the immigration check
    (B) Proceed to the baggage claim area
    (C) Call an ambulance
    (D) Report to the quarantine counter

(1 点×10)

Class	No.	Name	Score	/10

Unit 4 Outdoor Activities
~Let's go on an excursion! ~

☑ Point: 時間に関する表現

- ●8:30 (eight thirty / half past eight)
- ●9:50 (nine fifty / ten to ten)
- ●10:15 (ten fifteen / a quarter past ten)
- ●11:45 (eleven forty-five / a quarter to twelve)
- ●in time「間に合って」、on time「時間通りに」
- ●ahead of time「定刻より早く」、behind time「定刻より遅れて」
- ●on schedule「予定通りに」、~sharp「~ちょうど、きっかり」

📝 Warm-up Exercise: Asking for time　🎧 1-35

1. Do you have the time? ----- Well, it's about (　　　　　　).

2. What time shall we meet? ----- How about (　　　　　　) here?

3. Could you tell me what time our boarding starts?

　　　　　　　　　　　　　　　--- It was changed to (　　　　　　).

4. What is the departure time of this bus? ----- It departs at 9 (　　　　　　).

5. I'd like to start this game on time. ----- If so, we'd better meet here at (　　　　　　).

🗣 Mini-TOEIC® Listening

| Part 1 | Photographs | 🎧 1-36, 37 |

1.

(A) (B) (C) (D)

2.

(A) (B) (C) (D)

〈キリトリ線〉

3. Mark your answer on your answer sheet.   (A) (B) (C)
4. Mark your answer on your answer sheet.   (A) (B) (C)
5. Mark your answer on your answer sheet.   (A) (B) (C)
6. Mark your answer on your answer sheet.   (A) (B) (C)

Part 3   Short Conversation   CD 1-42, 43

7. What does the man have to do on Fridays?
(A) Go hiking
(B) Wake up early in the morning
(C) Work until late in the evening
(D) Go out with his friends

8. When will Katie and her friends get together for hiking?
(A) 11:30   (B) 11:45
(C) 12:00   (D) 12:15

Part 4   Short Talk   CD 1-44, 45

9. Look at the schedule. Which of the following steps has correct information?
(A) STEP 1
(B) STEP 2
(C) STEP 3
(D) STEP 4

	PLACE	TIME
STEP 1	Meeting at school	8:30
STEP 2	Departure time of bus	8:40
STEP 3	King's National Park	10:45
STEP 4	Arrival time at school	14:40

10. What does the man mean when he says, "don't miss it"?
(A) He implies that listeners have to be very punctual.
(B) He worries that he might forget something.
(C) He stresses that this event will be very exciting.
(D) He thinks that students will misunderstand this information.

(1 点×10)

Class	No.	Name	Score	/10

Unit 5 Weather
~Do you like the rainy season?~

✓ Point: 天気に関する表現

- weather forecast / weather report 「天気予報」
- temperature 「気温」 degrees (℃) 「～度」
- fair 「快晴の」 sunny 「晴れて」 cloudy 「曇って」 rainy 「雨が降って」 windy 「風が強くて」 snowy 「雪が降って」
- hot 「暑い」 warm 「暖かい」 humid 「蒸し暑い」 dry 「乾燥して」 freezing 「凍えそうに寒い」 cold 「寒い」 chilly 「肌寒い」 cool 「涼しい」
- typhoon 「台風」 lightning 「稲光」 thunder 「雷」 shower 「にわか雨」

📋 Warm-up Exercise: Describing weather   1-46

1. According to the weather (   ), it will be very (   ) tomorrow.

2. What's the weather (   ) in Tokyo now?
   ----- It's very cold and (   ) today.

3. It's a beautiful day, isn't it?
   ----- Yes, but there'll be some light (   ) this evening.

4. Is it the (   ) season now in Thailand?
   ----- Yeah. It's very hot and (   ).

5. What is the (   ) time of year in England?
   ----- I think it's spring. The (   ) temperature is around 22 degrees.

🧠 Mini-TOEIC® Listening

| Part 1 | Photographs | 1-47, 48

1.

(A) (B) (C) (D)

2.

(A) (B) (C) (D)

9

3. Mark your answer on your answer sheet.   (A) (B) (C)
4. Mark your answer on your answer sheet.   (A) (B) (C)
5. Mark your answer on your answer sheet.   (A) (B) (C)
6. Mark your answer on your answer sheet.   (A) (B) (C)

Part 3   **Short Conversation**   🎧 1-53, 54

7. What does Alex want to know?
   (A) The location of Seattle
   (B) The geography of Seattle
   (C) The climate of Seattle
   (D) The history of Seattle

8. How was the weather in Seattle in the summer?
   (A) Hot
   (B) Cold
   (C) Warm
   (D) Wet

Part 4   **Short Talk**   🎧 1-55, 56

9. What is tomorrow's highest temperature in Brisbane?
   (A) 23 degrees
   (B) 24 degrees
   (C) 27 degrees
   (D) 29 degrees

10. Look at the graphic. Choose the appropriate weather combinations in Cairns and Melbourne.
   (A) Weather 1 (Cairns) / Weather 3 (Melbourne)
   (B) Weather 2 (Cairns) / Weather 3 (Melbourne)
   (C) Weather 1 (Cairns) / Weather 4 (Melbourne)
   (D) Weather 2 (Cairns) / Weather 4 (Melbourne)

Weather 1	☀ ➡ ☁
Weather 2	🌦
Weather 3	☁
Weather 4	☔

(1 点×10)

Class	No.	Name	Score	/10

Unit 6 Holiday Plans
~What's on for your summer vacation?~

☑Point: 電話の会話に関する表現

- Hello, this is Ken speaking.「はい、ケンです」
- May I speak to X?「Xと話をしたいのですが」
- Please hold the line.「そのままお待ちください（保留にする）」
- hold on「電話をきらずに待つ」／ hang up「電話をきる」
- put you through to Y (connect you to Y)「あなたをYにつなぐ」
- (one's) line is busy now.「話し中です」
- Z is on another line.「Zは他の電話に出ています」
- cell phone / cellular phone / mobile phone「携帯電話」

📝Warm-up Exercise: Telephone conversations 💿 1-57

1. ABC Travel Agency. Jim (   ). ----- Hi, may I speak to Mr. Taylor?

2. Could you put me (   ) to Ms. Richards?
   ----- Sure. Please hold the (   ).

3. You can (   ) me on my (   ) phone anytime.
   ----- Thanks, that's great!

4. Hi, I'd like to talk to Mr. Lee.
   ----- He's on (   ) line now. Who is calling, please?

5. Would you like to (   ) a message? ----- No, I'll call him (   ).

🧠Mini-TOEIC® Listening

| Part 1 | Photographs | 💿 1-58, 59 |

1.

2.

(A) (B) (C) (D)   (A) (B) (C) (D)

1-60～63

3. Mark your answer on your answer sheet.   (A) (B) (C)
4. Mark your answer on your answer sheet.   (A) (B) (C)
5. Mark your answer on your answer sheet.   (A) (B) (C)
6. Mark your answer on your answer sheet.   (A) (B) (C)

Part 3   Short Conversation

1-64, 65

7. What will Yoshi do?
   (A) Go to the shopping mall
   (B) Pick up Elena in his car
   (C) Join Elena and Danielle if it's sunny
   (D) Show up another day

8. What is NOT mentioned in the conversation?
   (A) They will see each other at noon.
   (B) They will meet this weekend.
   (C) They will come by car.
   (D) They are all going shopping.

Part 4   Short Talk

1-66, 67

9. If you are looking for a place to stay, what should you do?
   (A) Stay on the line
   (B) Press 1
   (C) Press 2
   (D) Press 3

10. If you are interested in weekend travel, what should you do?
    (A) Stay on the line
    (B) Press 1
    (C) Press 2
    (D) Press 3

(1 点×10)

Class	No.	Name	Score	/10

〈 キリトリ線 〉

Unit 7 Resort Area
~Have a nice, relaxing time. ~

☑Point: 依頼に関する表現

- ●Could you do me a favor? 「お願いがあるのですが」
- ●May I ask a favor of you? 「お願いがあるのですが」
- ●Could you please ～? 「～していただけませんか」
- ●It would be great if you could ～. 「～して下さると有難いのですが」
- ●Would it be possible to request ～? 「～をお頼みするのは可能ですか」
- ●Do you mind ～ing? 「～していただいても構いませんか」
- ●I wonder if I could ～. 「～できるのかしら」

📝Warm-up Exercise: Requesting

💿 1-68

1. (   ) you show me some brochures for one-day trips, please? ----- Certainly.

2. I (   ) if I could (   ) Japanese yen into American dollars here.

3. Would it be possible to (   ) a twin room for tomorrow? I'd prefer non-smoking. ----- I'm sorry we're fully (   ).

4. It (   ) be great if you could (   ) a taxi to take me to the airport.

5. I'd just like to (   ) one thing: Do you (   ) carrying this luggage to my room?

🗣Mini-TOEIC® Listening

| Part 1 | Photographs |

💿 1-69, 70

1.

2.

(A) (B) (C) (D)   (A) (B) (C) (D)

3. Mark your answer on your answer sheet.   (A) (B) (C)
4. Mark your answer on your answer sheet.   (A) (B) (C)
5. Mark your answer on your answer sheet.   (A) (B) (C)
6. Mark your answer on your answer sheet.   (A) (B) (C)

Part 3   Short Conversation   🎧 CD 1-75, 76

Bellevue Hotel Room rates

	Standard room	Ocean-view room
Monday—Thursday	$150	$250
Friday—Sunday	$200	$300

7. Where is this conversation taking place?
   (A) The Bellevue Hotel   (B) The man's house
   (C) Victoria Island   (D) A travel agency

8. Look at the graphic. How much will they pay for the room?
   (A) $150   (B) $200
   (C) $250   (D) $300

Part 4   Short Talk   🎧 CD 1-77, 78

9. What does Port Macquarie boast?
   (A) Pebble beaches
   (B) Museums
   (C) Native animals
   (D) A cathedral

10. Which activity is NOT mentioned here?
   (A) Sea kayaking
   (B) Walking
   (C) Cruise
   (D) Barbecuing

(1 点×10)

Class	No.	Name		Score	/10

14

Unit 8 Directions

~Please tell me the way to this place.~

☑ **Point:** 場所案内に関する表現

- go straight down 「まっすぐ行く」 ●turn left at A 「A で左に曲がる」
- A is on your right 「A は右手にある（見えます）」 ●next to A 「A の隣」
- opposite A 「A の反対側」 ●behind A 「A の裏側」 ●in front of A 「A の前」
- between A and B 「A と B の間」 ●around the corner 「角を曲がった ところ」
- at the end of the corridor [hall] 「廊下の突き当たり」
- across the street from A 「A の向い側」 ●by way of A [via A] 「A を経由して」

📄 **Warm-up Exercise:** Asking for directions 1-79

1. Is there a bank around here? ----- Yes, there's one (　　　　　　　) this bookstore.

2. Could you tell me the way to Victoria Station? ----- Sure. Go straight (　　　　　　)
   this street and (　　　　　　) right at the park.

3. Excuse me, where is the closest post office? ----- It's just (　　　　　　) the corner.

4. I'm looking for the bus station to the city center. ----- There's one (　　　　　　) the
   street from that hotel.

5. How do I get to the Westside Hospital? ----- Walk to the (　　　　　　) of this block.
   You can see it on your (　　　　　　).

🧠 **Mini-TOEIC® Listening**

| Part 1 | Photographs | 1-80, 81 |

1.

(A) (B) (C) (D)

2.

(A) (B) (C) (D)

Part 2   Question-Response

3. Mark your answer on your answer sheet.   (A) (B) (C)
4. Mark your answer on your answer sheet.   (A) (B) (C)
5. Mark your answer on your answer sheet.   (A) (B) (C)
6. Mark your answer on your answer sheet.   (A) (B) (C)

Part 3   Short Conversation

7. What seems to be the man's problem?
   (A) He can't find the place where the interview will be.
   (B) He has too much time to kill.
   (C) He is very nervous about his interview.
   (D) He is looking for a coffee shop.

8. Look at the map. Where does the woman work?
   (A) Building A
   (B) Building B
   (C) Building C
   (D) Building D

Part 4   Short Talk

9. Where would you most likely hear this announcement?
   (A) At a bus stop
   (B) At a train station
   (C) At an airport
   (D) At a ferry terminal

10. How can you get to Richmond?
    (A) Change at Parramatta
    (B) Change at Town Hall
    (C) Change at Strathfield
    (D) Change at Hornsby

(1 点×10)

Class	No.	Name		Score	/10

Unit 9 Job Experience
~Do you have a part-time job?~

☑ Point: 資格・職業経験に関する用語

- job interview「就職の面接」 ●applicant「応募者」 ●job opening「求人」
- résumé / CV [curriculum vitae]「履歴書」 ●qualification「資格、資質、能力」
- position「役職」 ●requirement「必要条件」 ●condition / term「条件」
- hourly wage「時間給」 ●occupation「職業」 ●promotion「昇進」
- Personnel [Human Resources] Department「人事部」
- hire「～を雇う」 ●fire「～をクビにする」 ●apply for「～に応募する」
- be transferred to A「A へ転勤する」 ●be in charge of A「A 担当である」

📝 Warm-up Exercise: Asking about experience and qualifications 🎧 2-01

1. I'd like to (   ) for this position. ----- Then, please send your (   )
to the following address.

2. Please tell me about your (   ) working experience. ----- I used to work
for T&M Company, and I was in (   ) of customer service there.

3. How was the (   ) you interviewed today? ----- Well, not so bad.

4. Are you going to (   ) him? ----- I'd love to, but it depends on whether
he is (   ) with our working conditions.

5. I'm afraid the hourly (   ) that he requested is a bit high for his
(   ).

🧠 Mini-TOEIC® Listening

| Part 1 | Photographs | 🎧 2-02, 03 |

1.

(A) (B) (C) (D)

2.

(A) (B) (C) (D)

Part 2　Question-Response

 2-04～07

3. Mark your answer on your answer sheet.　(A) (B) (C)
4. Mark your answer on your answer sheet.　(A) (B) (C)
5. Mark your answer on your answer sheet.　(A) (B) (C)
6. Mark your answer on your answer sheet.　(A) (B) (C)

Part 3　Short Conversation

 2-08, 09

7. What kind of job is Lisa looking for?
   (A) Sales manager　　(B) Banker
   (C) Secretary　　　　(D) Librarian

8. What is Lisa good at?
   (A) Accounting　　　(B) Teaching
   (C) Designing　　　　(D) Relationship skills

Part 4　Short Talk

2-10, 11

JOB OPENINGS at AC&T!

We are hiring motivated people in the divisions below.
Technical Division··························· 5
General Affairs Division··············· 2
Accounting Division·······················1
Sales Division ······························· 10

9. Look at the graphic. How many people will be hired in this division?
   (A) One　　　　　(B) Two
   (C) Five　　　　　(D) Ten

10. Who will be given priority for this job position?
    (A) A person with practical experience
    (B) A person with insurance
    (C) A new graduate
    (D) A person who is good at deskwork

(1 点×10)

Class	No.	Name		Score	/10

18

Unit 10 Summer Sale
~Are you a bargain-hunter?~

☑ Point: 買い物に関する表現

> - purchase「購入（する）」 ●refund「返金（する）」 ●try on「試着する」
> - charge「(代金を)請求する、つけにする、クレジットカードで払う」
> - fitting room / dressing room「試着室」 ●consumption tax「消費税」
> - good buy「お買い得（品）」 ●buy one, get one free「1つ買えば1つ無料」
> - reasonable price「お買い得価格」 ●mark down「値下げする」
> - on sale「特価中、セール中」 ●on display「展示して、陳列して」 ●out of stock「在庫切れ」
> - cash「現金」 ●advertisement「広告、宣伝」

📄 Warm-up Exercise: Expressing preference   2-12

1. Would you like to (   ) it (   )? ----- Yes, where is the fitting room?

2. This T-shirt didn't fit. Could I exchange it or get a (   )? ----- Do you have a (   ) for that?

3. I'm looking for the new book written by Steven Jenkins. ----- I'm afraid it's out of (   ) at the moment.

4. How would you like to pay, by (   ) or charge? ----- Will you (   ) a VISA card?

5. How much does it cost? ----- That'll be $45.50 with (   ).

🧠 Mini-TOEIC® Listening

| Part 1 | Photographs | 2-13, 14 |

1.

2.

(A) (B) (C) (D)   (A) (B) (C) (D)

19

3. Mark your answer on your answer sheet.　(A) (B) (C)
4. Mark your answer on your answer sheet.　(A) (B) (C)
5. Mark your answer on your answer sheet.　(A) (B) (C)
6. Mark your answer on your answer sheet.　(A) (B) (C)

Part 3　Short Conversation

🎵 CD 2-19, 20

7. What is the man's opinion?
   (A) She looks better in blue.
   (B) She doesn't look good in either color.
   (C) The red T-shirt would look very good on her.
   (D) The red T-shirt is the best one of them all.

8. What will the woman do?
   (A) Ask for a smaller red T-shirt
   (B) Try on a blue T-shirt
   (C) Have the red T-shirt discounted
   (D) Exchange her T-shirt for the red one

Part 4　Short Talk

🎵 CD 2-21, 22

9. How much is a bag now?
   (A) $50　　　　(B) $65
   (C) $100　　　(D) $135

10. Look at the graphic. Which area offers another five percent discount for a limited time?
    (A) AREA 1
    (B) AREA 2
    (C) AREA 3
    (D) AREA 4

(1 点×10)

Class	No.	Name	Score	/10

〈キリトリ線〉

Unit 11 Restaurant
~Why don't we eat out today?~

☑ Point: 注文に関する表現

- A table for four, please. 「4人の席をお願いします」
- Could we have the menu, please? 「メニューをいただけますか」
- Are you ready to order? 「ご注文を承りましょうか」
- What is today's special? 「今日のおすすめ（特別料理）は何ですか」
- I'd recommend A. 「Aをおすすめいたします」
- Would you care for some dessert? 「デザートはいかがですか」
- May I have the check [bill], please? 「お勘定をお願いします」

📝 Warm-up Exercise: Ordering meals

 2-23

1. Are you (   ) to order now? ----- Yes, what's the soup of the (   )?

2. Could we book a table for (   ) at 7 tonight? We'd like a table near the window.

3. Is everything OK? ----- May I have (   ) (   ) bread?

4. Would you (   ) for some dessert?
   ----- No thanks. May I have the (   ), please?

5. How would you (   ) your steak (   )? ----- Medium-rare, please.

🧠 Mini-TOEIC® Listening

| Part 1 | Photographs |

🎧 2-24, 25

1.

(A) (B) (C) (D)

2.

(A) (B) (C) (D)

3. Mark your answer on your answer sheet.   (A) (B) (C)
4. Mark your answer on your answer sheet.   (A) (B) (C)
5. Mark your answer on your answer sheet.   (A) (B) (C)
6. Mark your answer on your answer sheet.   (A) (B) (C)

Part 3   Short Conversation

🎧 2-30, 31

7. What does the woman care about the most?
   (A) Price   (B) Speed
   (C) Amount   (D) Nutrition

8. Look at the menu. How much does the woman pay for her lunch?
   (A) $5.95
   (B) $6.00
   (C) $7.00
   (D) $9.75

Part 4   Short Talk

🎧 2-32, 33

9. Which pizza is the healthiest choice?
   (A) Mozzarella and Spinach
   (B) Seafood Special
   (C) Italian Veggie
   (D) Garlic Prawn

10. How can you get a soft drink for free?
    (A) By ordering a new pizza
    (B) By ordering two large pizzas
    (C) By ordering the Pizza & Pasta meal
    (D) By ordering some garlic bread

(1 点×10)

Class	No.	Name	Score	/10

Unit 12 Arts & Entertainment
~Do you prefer a museum to a movie?~

☑ Point: 感情に関する表現

- I feel like ～ ing. / I'm in the mood for ～ ing. 「～したい気分です」
- I am in a good (bad) mood. 「いい（良くない）気分です」
- I was moved. / I was impressed. 「感動しました」
- amazing / stunning 「驚くほど素晴らしい、見事な」
- breathtaking 「息をのむような、すごい」
- eye-opening 「目を見張るような、びっくりするような」
- disgusting 「気持ち悪い、うんざりさせるような」
- upset 「腹を立てて、気が動転して」 scary 「怖い」
- irritate 「怒らせる、イライラさせる」 annoy 「イライラさせる、困らせる」

📋 Warm-up Exercise: Explaining your feelings 💿 2-34

1. How was the movie you saw yesterday? ----- Great! I was really (   ) by the life of the main character.

2. I feel (   ) going somewhere this weekend. ----- Why (   ) we go to the New Orleans Jazz Festival this Saturday?

3. I had to wait 30 minutes in line at the National Museum. It was really (   ). ----- So, that's why you're not in a good (   ).

4. I happened to see Brad Pitt last week in Hollywood. It was (   )! I couldn't believe my (   ).

5. There are lots of (   ) art works in this exhibition. ----- Sounds good. Let's go see them.

🧠 Mini-TOEIC® Listening

Part 1   Photographs 💿 2-35, 36

1.

(A) (B) (C) (D)

2.

(A) (B) (C) (D)

2-37〜40

3. Mark your answer on your answer sheet.   (A) (B) (C)
4. Mark your answer on your answer sheet.   (A) (B) (C)
5. Mark your answer on your answer sheet.   (A) (B) (C)
6. Mark your answer on your answer sheet.   (A) (B) (C)

Part 3   Short Conversation
 2-41, 42

7. How does Judy feel about *The Godfather* movies?
   (A) She wonders if they're good enough.
   (B) They are good but too old.
   (C) They're disappointing and boring.
   (D) She likes them very much.

8. What does the woman mean when she says, "it depends"?
   (A) She wants to make negative comments on romantic comedies.
   (B) She thinks most romantic comedies are rather disappointing.
   (C) She hesitates to say that she likes *The Godfather*.
   (D) She implies that some romantic comedies do not fit her taste.

Part 4   Short Talk
2-43, 44

9. How much is a ticket for Tuesday afternoon?
   (A) £22
   (B) £24
   (C) £32
   (D) £42

10. If you are late for the performance, what are you expected to do?
    (A) Get a refund
    (B) Exchange a ticket for another
    (C) Find your seat during a break
    (D) Pay a fine

(1 点×10)

Class	No.	Name	Score	/10

Unit 13 Sports Events
~Which team are you going to support?~

☑ Point: スポーツに関する表現

- X won the game by 20 to 15. 「X がその試合に20 対15 で勝った」
- Y beat [defeated] Z 2-0 in the final game. 「決勝戦でY がZ を2 対0 で破った」
- break one's record 「〜の記録を破る」 ●cheer for A / support A 「A を応援する」
- It's not your fault. 「君のせいじゃないよ」 ●Never mind. 「気にするな」
- Go for it! 「頑張れ、それ行け！」 ●Well done! 「よくやった、お見事」
- We're almost [nearly] there. 「あともう一息だ」
- Give it a shot [try]! 「（試しに）やってみろよ」

📑 Warm-up Exercise: Sports and games

 2-45

1. Well (   )! He broke the world (   )! ----- Yeah, it was really amazing!
2. Did you hear the result of the World Cup final? ----- Yes. Germany (   ) Italy 3-0.
3. I really wanted him to (   ) this match. ----- It wasn't his (   ) he lost. He has a bad coach.
4. Come on! Go (   ) it! ----- Oh, no. He (   ) a good chance again!
5. What did you think about the Wimbledon semi-final? ----- It was a shame, really. I (   ) for Nadal, but he lost.

🎧 Mini-TOEIC® Listening

| Part 1 | Photographs | 2-46, 47 |

1.

(A) (B) (C) (D)

2.

(A) (B) (C) (D)

25

3. Mark your answer on your answer sheet.   (A) (B) (C)
4. Mark your answer on your answer sheet.   (A) (B) (C)
5. Mark your answer on your answer sheet.   (A) (B) (C)
6. Mark your answer on your answer sheet.   (A) (B) (C)

Part 3   Short Conversation   2-52, 53

7. Where was the woman last night?
   (A) At a library
   (B) At an arena
   (C) In front of a TV
   (D) At a theater

8. How did Ken Field play in the game?
   (A) He played actively and well.
   (B) He hit a home run.
   (C) He played basketball for a long time.
   (D) He missed some shots.

Part 4   Short Talk   2-54, 55

9. When did Italy last win the gold medal?
   (A) In 1966
   (B) In 1993
   (C) In 2003
   (D) In 2014

10. Who won the Olympic Gold in 2014?
    (A) Kiara DeVito
    (B) Mary Dion
    (C) Tatiana Myskina
    (D) Fiona Finch

(1 点×10)

Class	No.	Name	Score	/10

Unit 14 Having a Party
~Any ideas for Halloween or Thanksgiving?~

☑ Point: 感謝の気持ちを表す表現

- Thanks for the invitation. 「お誘い下さりありがとう」
- I appreciate your hospitality. 「おもてなしに感謝します」
- That's very kind of you. 「ご親切にどうも」
- I can't thank you enough. 「お礼の言いようもありません」
- I don't know what to say. 「お礼の言葉もありません」
- Thank you for everything. 「何かとお世話になりました」
- I'm very grateful to you for ～. 「あなたに～を大変感謝しています」
- I'd like to express my appreciation for ～. 「～に感謝したく思います」

📝 Warm-up Exercise: Expressing appreciation 💿 2-56

1. I can't ( ) you enough. ----- Don't ( ) it. Thanks for coming.
2. I really ( ) your hospitality. ----- It's my ( ).
3. Thanks for your ( ). We had a wonderful time. ----- You're very welcome.
4. Thank you for ( ) you've done for me. ----- The pleasure is ( ).
5. I'll never forget my time here. ----- That's very kind ( ) you.
   I ( ) you could stay longer.

🗣 Mini-TOEIC® Listening

Part 1	Photographs	💿 2-57, 58

1.

(A) (B) (C) (D)

2.

(A) (B) (C) (D)

3. Mark your answer on your answer sheet.   (A) (B) (C)
4. Mark your answer on your answer sheet.   (A) (B) (C)
5. Mark your answer on your answer sheet.   (A) (B) (C)
6. Mark your answer on your answer sheet.   (A) (B) (C)

Part 3   Short Conversation

2-63, 64

7. What is James going to do around Thanksgiving?
   (A) Return to his home
   (B) Go out with his friends
   (C) Invite the woman over for dinner
   (D) Visit the woman's house

8. What will the woman do on Thanksgiving Day?
   (A) Cook traditional cuisine
   (B) Buy a present for James
   (C) Order roast turkey from a restaurant
   (D) Eat out with James

Part 4   Short Talk

 2-65, 66

9. What do you have to bring to the party?
   (A) Your college friends   (B) Your student card
   (C) Your passport   (D) Your receipt

10. Look at the flyer. Which information needs to be corrected?
    (A) Location
    (B) Date
    (C) Dress-code
    (D) Telephone number

(1 点×10)

Class	No.	Name	Score	/10

Unit 15 Health
~Don't catch a cold! ~

☑ Point: 病気に関する表現

●headache「頭痛」 ●fever「熱」 ●hay fever「花粉症」 ●allergy「アレルギー」
●sore throat「喉の痛み」 ●cough「咳」 ●runny nose「鼻水」 ●symptom「症状」
●treatment「治療」 ●operation / surgery「手術」 ●surgeon「外科医」
●physician「医者（内科）」 ●GP [General Practitioner]「一般開業医（英国）」
●dentist「歯科医」 ●pharmacist「薬剤師」 ●prescription「処方箋」 ●patient「患者」
●insurance「保険」 ●pension「年金」

📄 Warm-up Exercise: Giving and getting advice 💿 2-67

1. Are you feeling OK? You don't look well. ----- I have a (   ) and a sore
   (   ).

2. I've got a terrible toothache. ----- You'd better see a (   ) as soon as possible.

3. Why don't you (   ) a few days (   ) work? ----- My doctor
   said that taking three (   ) of this medicine after every meal would be
   enough to (   ) me feel better.

4. The pharmacist recommends this medicine for my (   ).

5. In order to see a hospital (   ), you need to go to the reception desk to
   receive a visitor's (   ).

🧠 Mini-TOEIC® Listening

Part 1	Photographs	💿 2-68, 69

1.

(A) (B) (C) (D)

2.

(A) (B) (C) (D)

Part 2   Question-Response

3. Mark your answer on your answer sheet.   (A) (B) (C)
4. Mark your answer on your answer sheet.   (A) (B) (C)
5. Mark your answer on your answer sheet.   (A) (B) (C)
6. Mark your answer on your answer sheet.   (A) (B) (C)

Part 3   Short Conversation

7. What does Julie suggest that Joe should do?
(A) Explain to his boss
(B) Try not to catch a cold
(C) Go home
(D) Take some medicine

8. What will Sandra do after this?
(A) Tell Joe's boss about his situation
(B) Call her boss about a meeting
(C) Tell her boss to take a rest
(D) Send Joe a get-well card

Part 4   Short Talk

9. What does the National Health Service offer?
(A) A pension plan
(B) A mortgage plan
(C) A health insurance plan
(D) A student loan plan

10. Who CANNOT receive free treatment?
(A) EU citizens who stay for four months
(B) Japanese students who stay for three months
(C) British citizens
(D) American students who stay for seven months

(1 点×10)

Class	No.	Name		Score	/10

Christmas
~What are you wishing for on the day?~

☑ **Point:** 提案に関する表現

● Why don't you + [動詞の原形] ～? 「～するのはどうですか」
● What about ～ing? / How about ～ing? 「～するのはどうですか」
● Let's + [動詞の原形] ～. / Shall we + [動詞の原形] ～? 「～しましょう」
● Why not + [動詞の原形] ～? 「～してみればどうかな」
● You had better + [動詞の原形] ～. 「～したほうがよい」
● It might be better to ～. 「～するほうがよいかもしれない」
● I would rather + [動詞の原形] ～. 「むしろ～するほうがよい」

📝 **Warm-up Exercise:** **Making suggestions** 2-78

1. Why (   ) you take a friend to the party?----- That's a good idea. I'll ask Miki.
2. How (   ) going out for dinner tomorrow? ----- Sorry. I have (   ) appointment.
3. What shall I wear for the Christmas party? ----- Why (   ) try on this red dress?
4. We'd (   ) hurry up. ----- It (   ) be better to tell him that we'll be late.
5. Let's (   ) together this Sunday.
   ----- Great! What time (   ) we meet?

🧠 **Mini-TOEIC® Listening**

Part 1	Photographs	2-79, 80

1.

(A) (B) (C) (D)

2.

(A) (B) (C) (D)

3. Mark your answer on your answer sheet.   (A) (B) (C)
4. Mark your answer on your answer sheet.   (A) (B) (C)
5. Mark your answer on your answer sheet.   (A) (B) (C)
6. Mark your answer on your answer sheet.   (A) (B) (C)

Part 3   Short Conversation   2-85, 86

7. Where will the Christmas party be held?
   (A) Sarah's house
   (B) Ryo's house
   (C) A School
   (D) A Church

8. What will probably go well with the party?
   (A) Ryo's performance
   (B) Ryo's Japanese food
   (C) Candle service
   (D) Christmas carol

Part 4   Short Talk   2-87, 88

9. Where is this speech most likely taking place?
   (A) At a party
   (B) At an international conference
   (C) At a graduation ceremony
   (D) At a wedding

10. According to the speaker, what is the real meaning of Christmas?
    (A) To enjoy the festivities
    (B) To think about less fortunate people
    (C) To take care of your family
    (D) To be thankful for the food

(1 点×10)

Class	No.	Name	Score	/10

Unit 17 Cleanup
~Tidy up your house!~

☑ Point: 助けを求める・与える表現

- Could you give me a hand? 「手を貸していただけませんか」
- I need your help. 「手伝ってほしいのですが」
- Could you spare me a few minutes? 「ちょっとお時間よろしいですか」
- Let me help you. 「手伝わせてください」
- Can I help you with anything? 「何か手伝いましょうか」
- Is there anything I can do for you? 「何か私が出来ることはありますか」
- I'll be happy to assist you. 「喜んでお手伝いします」
- I'm glad [willing] to offer any assistance. 「喜んでお手伝いします」

📄 Warm-up Exercise: Asking for a favor and offering to help 💿 3-01

1. Can I help you (   ) anything?
        ----- You're my guest. (   ) yourself at home.
2. Please (   ) me help you.
        ----- Thanks. Could you wipe the (   ) with the cloth?
3. Would you (   ) me a few minutes? I need your (   ).
4. Could you (   ) me a hand? ----- Wow. Your room is really messy!
5. Do you (   ) washing the dishes after eating?
        ----- I'll be happy to (   ) you.

🧠 Mini-TOEIC® Listening

| Part 1 | Photographs | 💿 3-02, 03 |

1.

(A) (B) (C) (D)

2.

(A) (B) (C) (D)

33

Part 2   Question-Response

3. Mark your answer on your answer sheet.   (A) (B) (C)

4. Mark your answer on your answer sheet.   (A) (B) (C)

5. Mark your answer on your answer sheet.   (A) (B) (C)

6. Mark your answer on your answer sheet.   (A) (B) (C)

Part 3   Short Conversation

3-08, 09

7. What did the woman ask Kai to do?

(A) Vacuum the carpet

(B) Polish the furniture

(C) Wipe the windows

(D) Mop the stairs

8. What does the man mean when he says, "Don't mention it"?

(A) He thinks the woman is joking.

(B) He thinks he owes the woman a favor.

(C) He doesn't want to help the woman anymore.

(D) He doesn't think that he deserves her appreciation.

Part 4   Short Talk

3-10, 11

9. Look at the graphic. On which day does Lindsay have to take out the garbage?

(A) Thursday, December 24th

(B) Monday, December 28th

(C) Wednesday, December 30th

(D) Thursday, December 31st

December						
Sun	Mon	Tue	Wed	Thu	Fri	Sat
				24	25	26
27	28	29	30	31		

10. What is Lindsay asked to do?

(A) To bring in the newspaper

(B) To feed the cat

(C) To open and check all letters

(D) To water the plants every other day

(1 点×10)

Class	No.	Name		Score	/10

キリトリ線

34

Unit 18 Our Traditions & Customs
~How do you celebrate the New Year?~

☑ Point: 人物描写や位置関係を説明する表現

●tall「背が高い」 ●short「背が低い」 ●chubby「小太りな」 ●thin「痩せて」
●skinny「痩せて」 ●slim「すらっとした、ほっそりした」 ●curly「巻き毛の」
●short straight「短くまっすぐな」 ●long wavy「長くウェーブのかかった」
●tie back one's hair「髪の毛を後ろでまとめる」
●wear one's hair down「髪の毛を下ろしている」 ●side by side「並んで、隣り合って」
●face to face「向かい合って」 ●upside down「逆さまの」 ●beside A「Aの傍らに」
●in (a) line「列になって」 ●line up「1列に並ぶ」 ●pile up「積み重なる」

📝 Warm-up Exercise: Describing people and locations 🎧 3-12

1. Look at the woman in a kimono with long (　　　　　) hair!
   ----- Wow! She looks really traditional.
2. Many people are waiting in (　　　　) to (　　　　) a wish for the New Year. ----- Yes. This is our custom.
3. You should not put these two things side (　　　　) side. ----- That's OK. I'm not superstitious.
4. I think I gained some (　　　　) during the winter holidays.
   ----- Don't worry! You're still so (　　　　).
5. Do you know why these sculptures are standing face (　　　　) face?
   ----- I'm not sure, but there might be some (　　　　) reasons.

🧠 Mini-TOEIC® Listening

| Part 1 | Photographs | 🎧 3-13, 14 |

1.

(A) (B) (C) (D)

2.

(A) (B) (C) (D)

3. Mark your answer on your answer sheet.   (A) (B) (C)
4. Mark your answer on your answer sheet.   (A) (B) (C)
5. Mark your answer on your answer sheet.   (A) (B) (C)
6. Mark your answer on your answer sheet.   (A) (B) (C)

Part 3   Short Conversation 3-19, 20

7. Why does Yuko like to wear a kimono?
   (A) Because it fits her body
   (B) Because it's not so heavy
   (C) Because it helps keep her health good
   (D) Because her mother likes kimonos

8. How does Yuko get dressed in a kimono?
   (A) She always puts it on by herself.
   (B) She helps her mother get into it.
   (C) Her mother helps her to put it on.
   (D) She goes to a beauty shop to put it on.

Part 4   Short Talk 3-21, 22

9. How does the man learn about Japanese culture?
   (A) From his siblings
   (B) From his father
   (C) From his mother
   (D) From his extended family

10. What does the man do on New Year's Day?
    (A) Eat rice-cake soup
    (B) Visit a temple or shrine
    (C) Make rice cakes
    (D) Visit his relatives in Japan

（1 点×10）

Class	No.	Name		Score	/10

〈 キ リ ト リ 線 〉

Unit 19 Examinations

~When is the deadline for this assignment?~

☑ Point: 条件・日程に関する用語

- submit / hand in / turn in「～を提出する」 ● postpone / put off「～を延期する」
- extend「～を延長する」 ● expire「(予定)期日を過ぎる、有効期限が切れる」
- attend「～に出席する」 ● fail「(テスト)に落ちる、落第する」〔⇔ pass〕
- deadline「締切り、最終期日」 ● due date「締切日、予定日、返却日」
- appointment「約束、予約」 ● assignment「課題、宿題」 ● credit / unit「単位」
- GPA [Grade Point Average]「(学校の)成績平均値」 ● transcript「成績証明書」
- within two weeks「2週間以内に」 ● by the end of this month「今月末までに」
- until March 31st / the 31st of March「3月31日まで」

📋 Warm-up Exercise: Dates and conditions   3-23

1. You need to (   ) this assignment to my office (   ) the end of this week.

2. What's the matter? ----- I'd like to ask you to (   ) the deadline of this report (   ) June 15th.

3. I'd like to check out these books. ----- Sure. The (   ) date is the 11th of May.

4. How was your final exam in politics? ----- I'm afraid I might (   ) the class.

5. Could I make an (   ) for tomorrow's seminar? ----- It was (   ) to next Friday.

🧠 Mini-TOEIC® Listening

| Part 1 | Photographs | 3-24, 25 |

1.

(A) (B) (C) (D)

2.

(A) (B) (C) (D)

3. Mark your answer on your answer sheet.   (A) (B) (C)
4. Mark your answer on your answer sheet.   (A) (B) (C)
5. Mark your answer on your answer sheet.   (A) (B) (C)
6. Mark your answer on your answer sheet.   (A) (B) (C)

Part 3   Short Conversation   3-30, 31

7. What did the professor recommend the woman to do?
   (A) Extend her deadline
   (B) Take a make-up class
   (C) Submit an extra report
   (D) Read reference books

8. What does the woman want from the professor?
   (A) Permission to miss the next three classes
   (B) More time to complete her paper
   (C) A make-up class to help her catch up
   (D) All the reference books

Part 4   Short Talk   3-32, 33

9. Who is most likely the speaker?
   (A) A venture capitalist
   (B) A computer company employee
   (C) A director of a museum
   (D) A college professor

10. What is the speaker asking people to do in the first week of January?
   (A) Submit a report
   (B) Give a presentation
   (C) Sit for an exam
   (D) Hand in a final essay

(1 点×10)

Class	No.	Name		Score	/10

Unit 20 Housing

~I'm looking for a new apartment.~

☑ Point: 数字と交渉表現

- ●sign the contract「契約に署名する」 ●accept the condition「条件を受け入れる」
- ●come to a conclusion「結論を出す」 ●reach an agreement「合意に達する」
- ●meet one's request「要望にこたえる」 ●get a mortgage「住宅ローンを組む」
- ●guarantee「保証（する）、保証人（となる）」 ●warranty「保証」
- ●one trillion「1兆」 ●three billion「30億」 ●two hundred million「2億」
- ●ten million「1千万（10,000,000）」 ●five million「5百万（5,000,000）」
- ●twenty thousand「2万」
- ●one point five「1.5」 ●forty-five point twenty-five「45.25」

📋 Warm-up Exercise: Negotiating and numbers 3-34

1. You need to sign this (   ) when you move into this university dormitory.
   ----- I understand.

2. Forty-thousand yen would be the limit for my monthly (   ).
   ----- I'll try to find an apartment which (   ) your request.

3. My family decided to (   ) a mortgage in order to buy this property.
   ----- I think it's a good investment.

4. We finally (   ) to the conclusion that we would move to California next
   year. ----- I envy you!

5. The real estate agent (   ) our condition to sell our house for more than 50
   (   ) dollars.

🎧 Mini-TOEIC® Listening

| Part 1 | Photographs | 3-35, 36 |

(A) (B) (C) (D)

(A) (B) (C) (D)

3. Mark your answer on your answer sheet.   (A) (B) (C)
4. Mark your answer on your answer sheet.   (A) (B) (C)
5. Mark your answer on your answer sheet.   (A) (B) (C)
6. Mark your answer on your answer sheet.   (A) (B) (C)

Part 3   Short Conversation 3-41, 42

7. Who is Mr. Cooper talking to?
   (A) Mr. and Mrs. Cooper's friend
   (B) Mr. Cooper's sister
   (C) A real estate agent
   (D) A financial planner

8. Which is NOT mentioned in this conversation?
   (A) Mr. and Mrs. Cooper have hesitated to buy a house.
   (B) Mr. and Mrs. Cooper are concerned about the current economic situation.
   (C) The woman encourages Mr. and Mrs. Cooper to buy a house.
   (D) The woman has decided to buy a house at a low interest rate.

Part 4   Short Talk   3-43, 44

9. What should students do before choosing their accommodations?
   (A) Meet the landlord
   (B) Lock up the house
   (C) Check the location of the property
   (D) Pay a deposit

10. After deciding where to live, what do students need to do first?
    (A) Pay a deposit
    (B) Pay two weeks' worth of rent
    (C) Submit an application
    (D) Sign an agreement

(1点×10)

Class	No.	Name	Score	/10

Review Test 1

Unit 1-5

[Ceremony, School Life, Transportation, Outdoor Activities, Weather]

| Part 1 | Photographs | 3-45~48 |

1.

(A) (B) (C) (D)

2.

(A) (B) (C) (D)

3.

(A) (B) (C) (D)

4.

(A) (B) (C) (D)

| Part 2 | Question-Response | 3-49~53 |

5. Mark your answer on your answer sheet.   (A) (B) (C)
6. Mark your answer on your answer sheet.   (A) (B) (C)
7. Mark your answer on your answer sheet.   (A) (B) (C)
8. Mark your answer on your answer sheet.   (A) (B) (C)
9. Mark your answer on your answer sheet.   (A) (B) (C)

10. Look at the graphic. Which of the following students is probably Aiko?

(A) Student A

(B) Student B

(C) Student C

(D) Student D

	Electives	Required subjects
STUDENT A	3	5
STUDENT B	5	8
STUDENT C	8	10
STUDENT D	10	13

11. When is the conversation probably taking place?

(A) In the middle of winter vacation

(B) At the beginning of the semester

(C) At the end of the semester

(D) At the graduation ceremony

12. How many credits are at least necessary for their graduation?

(A) 30   (B) 80

(C) 100   (D) 120

13. Where should students return books during the day?

(A) To the shelves

(B) In the return box

(C) To the new checkout machine

(D) At a desk on level 2

14. If students have overdue books, what do they have to do?

(A) Pay a fine

(B) Return their library card

(C) Return books in the box immediately

(D) Contact the library staff via e-mail

15. When are library tours offered?

(A) Throughout the year

(B) The first few weeks of each semester

(C) The first few weeks of each year

(D) The first week of each semester

（1 点×15）

Class	No.	Name	Score	/15

〈キリトリ線〉

Review Test 2

Unit 6-10

[Holiday Plans, Resort Area, Directions, Job Experience, Summer Sale]

1.

(A) (B) (C) (D)

2.

(A) (B) (C) (D)

3.

(A) (B) (C) (D)

4.

(A) (B) (C) (D)

Part 2   Question-Response   3-62~66

5. Mark your answer on your answer sheet.   (A) (B) (C)

6. Mark your answer on your answer sheet.   (A) (B) (C)

7. Mark your answer on your answer sheet.   (A) (B) (C)

8. Mark your answer on your answer sheet.   (A) (B) (C)

9. Mark your answer on your answer sheet.   (A) (B) (C)

Part 3   Short Conversation

10. When is the conversation taking place?
    (A) Early spring   (B) Early summer
    (C) Late summer   (D) Early fall

11. Where will the woman probably spend her holidays?
    (A) Outside   (B) At the beach
    (C) At home   (D) In Hawaii

12. What are they probably going to do together?
    (A) Visit friends in Hawaii
    (B) Study for examinations
    (C) Hold a party
    (D) Enjoy diving in the sea

Part 4   Short Talk

13. What time is the summer event held?
    (A) 12:00 -12:20
    (B) 12:20 -13:00
    (C) 13:00 -13:20
    (D) 14:00 -14:20

14. Where do you need to go to see the fashion show?
    (A) Outside the shopping center
    (B) In front of the food court
    (C) Next to the ABC Photo Shop
    (D) In the Waterfall Bookstore

15. What kind of special privilege can people earn at the event?
    (A) Free food
    (B) Free drink
    (C) Free trip to a resort area
    (D) Free product

(1 点×15)

Class	No.	Name		Score	/15

Review Test 3

Unit 11-15

[Restaurant, Arts & Entertainment, Sports Events, Having a Party, Health]

1.

(A) (B) (C) (D)

2.

(A) (B) (C) (D)

3.

(A) (B) (C) (D)

4.

(A) (B) (C) (D)

5. Mark your answer on your answer sheet.   (A) (B) (C)
6. Mark your answer on your answer sheet.   (A) (B) (C)
7. Mark your answer on your answer sheet.   (A) (B) (C)
8. Mark your answer on your answer sheet.   (A) (B) (C)
9. Mark your answer on your answer sheet.   (A) (B) (C)

10. How does Mia describe Halloween in her town?
    (A) It is very special.
    (B) It is frightening.
    (C) It is tricky.
    (D) It is conventional.

11. What is a "jack-o'-lantern" ?
    (A) A unique costume
    (B) A big orange cake
    (C) A lamp made of a pumpkin
    (D) A famous Halloween song

12. Why do people give the children store-bought treats lately?
    (A) Because it is difficult to trust handmade goodies.
    (B) Because store-bought candies taste much better.
    (C) Because it costs too much to bake cookies at home.
    (D) Because it is more convenient for stores to deliver all the candies.

Part 4 | Short Talk   🔊 3-82, 83

13. What does the man mean when he says, "I'll tell you all the points from A to Z"?
    (A) He wants to speak with every student in person.
    (B) He will guide students to the place where they can meet a GP.
    (C) He will explain all the important things about how to register with a GP.
    (D) He will talk about all the abbreviations such as GP and NHS.

14. What will students need to bring on their first visit to a GP?
    (A) A passport
    (B) A library card
    (C) Proof of residence in their home country
    (D) A credit card

15. What service is NOT covered by the NHS?
    (A) Vaccination
    (B) Family planning
    (C) Treatment for serious diseases
    (D) Treatment for a cold

〈キリトリ線〉

(1 点×15)

Class	No.	Name	Score	/15

Review Test 4

Unit 16-20

[Christmas, Cleanup, Our Traditions & Customs, Examinations, Housing]

1.

(A) (B) (C) (D)

2.

(A) (B) (C) (D)

3.

(A) (B) (C) (D)

4.

(A) (B) (C) (D)

---

5. Mark your answer on your answer sheet.   (A) (B) (C)
6. Mark your answer on your answer sheet.   (A) (B) (C)
7. Mark your answer on your answer sheet.   (A) (B) (C)
8. Mark your answer on your answer sheet.   (A) (B) (C)
9. Mark your answer on your answer sheet.   (A) (B) (C)

Part 3   Short Conversation   3-93, 94

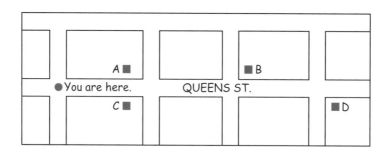

10. Look at the map. Which of the following buildings probably is a post office?

(A) Building A   (B) Building B   (C) Building C   (D) Building D

11. Where is the woman's final destination?

(A) Post Office   (B) Job Center   (C) Estate Office   (D) Convenience Store

12. Which of the following is true?

(A) The color of the post office building is black.

(B) The woman is in a hurry for a job interview.

(C) Century Housing seems to be relatively a new office.

(D) The woman left her mobile phone at home.

Part 4   Short Talk   3-95, 96

13. Who invented the Caesar salad?

(A) Julius Caesar   (B) An Italian immigrant

(C) A Mexican chef   (D) A foreign tourist

14. Which ingredient is NOT included in Caesar salad?

(A) Garlic   (B) Olive Oil

(C) Ginger   (D) Parmesan cheese

15. Why was the restaurant closed in the end?

(A) Violence   (B) Drugs

(C) Recession   (D) Illness

(1 点×15)

Class	No.	Name	Score	/15

TEXT PRODUCTION STAFF

edited by	編集
Taiichi Sano	佐野 泰一
Eiichi Tamura	田村 栄一

English-language editing by	英文校閲
Bill Benfield	ビル・ベンフィールド

cover design by	表紙デザイン
Nobuyoshi Fujino	藤野 伸芳

text design by	本文デザイン
Hiroyuki Kinouchi(ALIUS)	木野内 宏行 (アリウス)

CD PRODUCTION STAFF

narrated by	吹き込み者
Chris Koprowski (AmE)	クリス・コプロスキー (アメリカ英語)
Rachel Walzer (AmE)	レイチェル・ウォルザー (アメリカ英語)
Nadia Mckechnie (BrE)	ナディア・マケックニー (イギリス英語)
Andree Dufleit (CanE)	アンドリュー・デュフレイ (カナダ英語)
Brad Homes (AusE)	ブラッド・ホームズ (オーストラリア英語)
Howard Colefield (AmE)	ハワード・コールフィールド (アメリカ英語)
Karen Haedrich (AmE)	カレン・ヘドリック (アメリカ英語)
Guy Perryman (BrE)	ガイ・ペリマン (イギリス英語)
Sarah Greaves (AusE)	サラ・グリーブス (オーストラリア英語)
Neil DeMaere (CanE)	ニール・デマル (カナダ英語)

PRACTICAL SITUATIONS FOR THE TOEIC® TEST LISTENING
─Revised Edition─
実生活で役立つTOEIC® テストリスニング ─改訂新版─

2020年1月20日　初版発行
2024年2月10日　第6刷発行

著　　者　　吉田 佳代
　　　　　　仲西 恭子
　　　　　　板垣 静香
　　　　　　Brian Covert

発 行 者　　佐野 英一郎

発 行 所　　株式会社 成 美 堂
　　　　　　〒101-0052　東京都千代田区神田小川町3-22
　　　　　　TEL 03-3291-2261　FAX 03-3293-5490
　　　　　　https://www.seibido.co.jp

印 刷　　(株)倉敷印刷
製 本　　(株)倉敷印刷

ISBN 978-4-7919-7215-9　　　　　　　　　　　　Printed in Japan

Unit 1	Part 1	Part 2	Part 3	Part 4
	1. Ⓐ Ⓑ Ⓒ Ⓓ	3. Ⓐ Ⓑ Ⓒ	7. Ⓐ Ⓑ Ⓒ Ⓓ	9. Ⓐ Ⓑ Ⓒ Ⓓ
	2. Ⓐ Ⓑ Ⓒ Ⓓ	4. Ⓐ Ⓑ Ⓒ	8. Ⓐ Ⓑ Ⓒ Ⓓ	10. Ⓐ Ⓑ Ⓒ Ⓓ
		5. Ⓐ Ⓑ Ⓒ		
		6. Ⓐ Ⓑ Ⓒ		

Class _____ No _____ Name _____ Score _____ /10

Unit 2	Part 1	Part 2	Part 3	Part 4
	1. Ⓐ Ⓑ Ⓒ Ⓓ	3. Ⓐ Ⓑ Ⓒ	7. Ⓐ Ⓑ Ⓒ Ⓓ	9. Ⓐ Ⓑ Ⓒ Ⓓ
	2. Ⓐ Ⓑ Ⓒ Ⓓ	4. Ⓐ Ⓑ Ⓒ	8. Ⓐ Ⓑ Ⓒ Ⓓ	10. Ⓐ Ⓑ Ⓒ Ⓓ
		5. Ⓐ Ⓑ Ⓒ		
		6. Ⓐ Ⓑ Ⓒ		

Class _____ No _____ Name _____ Score _____ /10

Unit 3	Part 1	Part 2	Part 3	Part 4
	1. Ⓐ Ⓑ Ⓒ Ⓓ	3. Ⓐ Ⓑ Ⓒ	7. Ⓐ Ⓑ Ⓒ Ⓓ	9. Ⓐ Ⓑ Ⓒ Ⓓ
	2. Ⓐ Ⓑ Ⓒ Ⓓ	4. Ⓐ Ⓑ Ⓒ	8. Ⓐ Ⓑ Ⓒ Ⓓ	10. Ⓐ Ⓑ Ⓒ Ⓓ
		5. Ⓐ Ⓑ Ⓒ		
		6. Ⓐ Ⓑ Ⓒ		

Class _____ No _____ Name _____ Score _____ /10

〈キ リ ト リ 線〉

Unit 4	Part 1	Part 2	Part 3	Part 4
	1. Ⓐ Ⓑ Ⓒ Ⓓ	3. Ⓐ Ⓑ Ⓒ	7. Ⓐ Ⓑ Ⓒ Ⓓ	9. Ⓐ Ⓑ Ⓒ Ⓓ
	2. Ⓐ Ⓑ Ⓒ Ⓓ	4. Ⓐ Ⓑ Ⓒ	8. Ⓐ Ⓑ Ⓒ Ⓓ	10. Ⓐ Ⓑ Ⓒ Ⓓ
		5. Ⓐ Ⓑ Ⓒ		
		6. Ⓐ Ⓑ Ⓒ		

Class _____ No _____ Name _____ Score _____ /10

Unit 5	Part 1	Part 2	Part 3	Part 4
	1. Ⓐ Ⓑ Ⓒ Ⓓ	3. Ⓐ Ⓑ Ⓒ	7. Ⓐ Ⓑ Ⓒ Ⓓ	9. Ⓐ Ⓑ Ⓒ Ⓓ
	2. Ⓐ Ⓑ Ⓒ Ⓓ	4. Ⓐ Ⓑ Ⓒ	8. Ⓐ Ⓑ Ⓒ Ⓓ	10. Ⓐ Ⓑ Ⓒ Ⓓ
		5. Ⓐ Ⓑ Ⓒ		
		6. Ⓐ Ⓑ Ⓒ		

Class _____ No _____ Name _____ Score _____ /10

Unit 6	Part 1	Part 2	Part 3	Part 4
	1. Ⓐ Ⓑ Ⓒ Ⓓ	3. Ⓐ Ⓑ Ⓒ	7. Ⓐ Ⓑ Ⓒ Ⓓ	9. Ⓐ Ⓑ Ⓒ Ⓓ
	2. Ⓐ Ⓑ Ⓒ Ⓓ	4. Ⓐ Ⓑ Ⓒ	8. Ⓐ Ⓑ Ⓒ Ⓓ	10. Ⓐ Ⓑ Ⓒ Ⓓ
		5. Ⓐ Ⓑ Ⓒ		
		6. Ⓐ Ⓑ Ⓒ		

Class _____ No _____ Name _____ Score _____ /10

Unit 7	Part 1	Part 2	Part 3	Part 4
	1. Ⓐ Ⓑ Ⓒ Ⓓ	3. Ⓐ Ⓑ Ⓒ	7. Ⓐ Ⓑ Ⓒ Ⓓ	9. Ⓐ Ⓑ Ⓒ Ⓓ
	2. Ⓐ Ⓑ Ⓒ Ⓓ	4. Ⓐ Ⓑ Ⓒ	8. Ⓐ Ⓑ Ⓒ Ⓓ	10. Ⓐ Ⓑ Ⓒ Ⓓ
		5. Ⓐ Ⓑ Ⓒ		
		6. Ⓐ Ⓑ Ⓒ		

Class _____ No _____ Name _____ Score _____ /10

Unit 8	Part 1	Part 2	Part 3	Part 4
	1. Ⓐ Ⓑ Ⓒ Ⓓ	3. Ⓐ Ⓑ Ⓒ	7. Ⓐ Ⓑ Ⓒ Ⓓ	9. Ⓐ Ⓑ Ⓒ Ⓓ
	2. Ⓐ Ⓑ Ⓒ Ⓓ	4. Ⓐ Ⓑ Ⓒ	8. Ⓐ Ⓑ Ⓒ Ⓓ	10. Ⓐ Ⓑ Ⓒ Ⓓ
		5. Ⓐ Ⓑ Ⓒ		
		6. Ⓐ Ⓑ Ⓒ		

Class _____ No _____ Name _____ Score _____ /10

Unit 9	Part 1	Part 2	Part 3	Part 4
	1. Ⓐ Ⓑ Ⓒ Ⓓ	3. Ⓐ Ⓑ Ⓒ	7. Ⓐ Ⓑ Ⓒ Ⓓ	9. Ⓐ Ⓑ Ⓒ Ⓓ
	2. Ⓐ Ⓑ Ⓒ Ⓓ	4. Ⓐ Ⓑ Ⓒ	8. Ⓐ Ⓑ Ⓒ Ⓓ	10. Ⓐ Ⓑ Ⓒ Ⓓ
		5. Ⓐ Ⓑ Ⓒ		
		6. Ⓐ Ⓑ Ⓒ		

Class _____ No _____ Name _____ Score _____ /10

Unit 10	Part 1	Part 2	Part 3	Part 4
	1. Ⓐ Ⓑ Ⓒ Ⓓ	3. Ⓐ Ⓑ Ⓒ	7. Ⓐ Ⓑ Ⓒ Ⓓ	9. Ⓐ Ⓑ Ⓒ Ⓓ
	2. Ⓐ Ⓑ Ⓒ Ⓓ	4. Ⓐ Ⓑ Ⓒ	8. Ⓐ Ⓑ Ⓒ Ⓓ	10. Ⓐ Ⓑ Ⓒ Ⓓ
		5. Ⓐ Ⓑ Ⓒ		
		6. Ⓐ Ⓑ Ⓒ		

Class _____ No _____ Name _____ Score _____ /10

Unit 11	Part 1	Part 2	Part 3	Part 4
	1. Ⓐ Ⓑ Ⓒ Ⓓ	3. Ⓐ Ⓑ Ⓒ	7. Ⓐ Ⓑ Ⓒ Ⓓ	9. Ⓐ Ⓑ Ⓒ Ⓓ
	2. Ⓐ Ⓑ Ⓒ Ⓓ	4. Ⓐ Ⓑ Ⓒ	8. Ⓐ Ⓑ Ⓒ Ⓓ	10. Ⓐ Ⓑ Ⓒ Ⓓ
		5. Ⓐ Ⓑ Ⓒ		
		6. Ⓐ Ⓑ Ⓒ		

Class _____ No _____ Name _____ Score _____ /10

Unit 12	Part 1	Part 2	Part 3	Part 4
	1. Ⓐ Ⓑ Ⓒ Ⓓ	3. Ⓐ Ⓑ Ⓒ	7. Ⓐ Ⓑ Ⓒ Ⓓ	9. Ⓐ Ⓑ Ⓒ Ⓓ
	2. Ⓐ Ⓑ Ⓒ Ⓓ	4. Ⓐ Ⓑ Ⓒ	8. Ⓐ Ⓑ Ⓒ Ⓓ	10. Ⓐ Ⓑ Ⓒ Ⓓ
		5. Ⓐ Ⓑ Ⓒ		
		6. Ⓐ Ⓑ Ⓒ		

Class _____ No _____ Name _____ Score _____ /10

〈キリトリ線〉

Unit 13	Part 1	Part 2	Part 3	Part 4
	1. Ⓐ Ⓑ Ⓒ Ⓓ	3. Ⓐ Ⓑ Ⓒ	7. Ⓐ Ⓑ Ⓒ Ⓓ	9. Ⓐ Ⓑ Ⓒ Ⓓ
	2. Ⓐ Ⓑ Ⓒ Ⓓ	4. Ⓐ Ⓑ Ⓒ	8. Ⓐ Ⓑ Ⓒ Ⓓ	10. Ⓐ Ⓑ Ⓒ Ⓓ
		5. Ⓐ Ⓑ Ⓒ		
		6. Ⓐ Ⓑ Ⓒ		

Class _____ No _____ Name _____ Score _____ /10

Unit 14	Part 1	Part 2	Part 3	Part 4
	1. Ⓐ Ⓑ Ⓒ Ⓓ	3. Ⓐ Ⓑ Ⓒ	7. Ⓐ Ⓑ Ⓒ Ⓓ	9. Ⓐ Ⓑ Ⓒ Ⓓ
	2. Ⓐ Ⓑ Ⓒ Ⓓ	4. Ⓐ Ⓑ Ⓒ	8. Ⓐ Ⓑ Ⓒ Ⓓ	10. Ⓐ Ⓑ Ⓒ Ⓓ
		5. Ⓐ Ⓑ Ⓒ		
		6. Ⓐ Ⓑ Ⓒ		

Class _____ No _____ Name _____ Score _____ /10

Unit 15	Part 1	Part 2	Part 3	Part 4
	1. Ⓐ Ⓑ Ⓒ Ⓓ	3. Ⓐ Ⓑ Ⓒ	7. Ⓐ Ⓑ Ⓒ Ⓓ	9. Ⓐ Ⓑ Ⓒ Ⓓ
	2. Ⓐ Ⓑ Ⓒ Ⓓ	4. Ⓐ Ⓑ Ⓒ	8. Ⓐ Ⓑ Ⓒ Ⓓ	10. Ⓐ Ⓑ Ⓒ Ⓓ
		5. Ⓐ Ⓑ Ⓒ		
		6. Ⓐ Ⓑ Ⓒ		

Class _____ No _____ Name _____ Score _____ /10

Unit 16	Part 1	Part 2	Part 3	Part 4
	1. Ⓐ Ⓑ Ⓒ Ⓓ	3. Ⓐ Ⓑ Ⓒ	7. Ⓐ Ⓑ Ⓒ Ⓓ	9. Ⓐ Ⓑ Ⓒ Ⓓ
	2. Ⓐ Ⓑ Ⓒ Ⓓ	4. Ⓐ Ⓑ Ⓒ	8. Ⓐ Ⓑ Ⓒ Ⓓ	10. Ⓐ Ⓑ Ⓒ Ⓓ
		5. Ⓐ Ⓑ Ⓒ		
		6. Ⓐ Ⓑ Ⓒ		

Class _____ No _____ Name _____ Score _____ /10

Unit 17	Part 1	Part 2	Part 3	Part 4
	1. Ⓐ Ⓑ Ⓒ Ⓓ	3. Ⓐ Ⓑ Ⓒ	7. Ⓐ Ⓑ Ⓒ Ⓓ	9. Ⓐ Ⓑ Ⓒ Ⓓ
	2. Ⓐ Ⓑ Ⓒ Ⓓ	4. Ⓐ Ⓑ Ⓒ	8. Ⓐ Ⓑ Ⓒ Ⓓ	10. Ⓐ Ⓑ Ⓒ Ⓓ
		5. Ⓐ Ⓑ Ⓒ		
		6. Ⓐ Ⓑ Ⓒ		

Class _____ No _____ Name _____ Score _____ /10

Unit 18	Part 1	Part 2	Part 3	Part 4
	1. Ⓐ Ⓑ Ⓒ Ⓓ	3. Ⓐ Ⓑ Ⓒ	7. Ⓐ Ⓑ Ⓒ Ⓓ	9. Ⓐ Ⓑ Ⓒ Ⓓ
	2. Ⓐ Ⓑ Ⓒ Ⓓ	4. Ⓐ Ⓑ Ⓒ	8. Ⓐ Ⓑ Ⓒ Ⓓ	10. Ⓐ Ⓑ Ⓒ Ⓓ
		5. Ⓐ Ⓑ Ⓒ		
		6. Ⓐ Ⓑ Ⓒ		

Class _____ No _____ Name _____ Score _____ /10

〈キ リ ト リ 線〉

Unit 19	Part 1	Part 2	Part 3	Part 4		
	1. Ⓐ Ⓑ Ⓒ Ⓓ	3. Ⓐ Ⓑ Ⓒ	7. Ⓐ Ⓑ Ⓒ Ⓓ	9. Ⓐ Ⓑ Ⓒ Ⓓ		
	2. Ⓐ Ⓑ Ⓒ Ⓓ	4. Ⓐ Ⓑ Ⓒ	8. Ⓐ Ⓑ Ⓒ Ⓓ	10. Ⓐ Ⓑ Ⓒ Ⓓ		
		5. Ⓐ Ⓑ Ⓒ				
		6. Ⓐ Ⓑ Ⓒ				
	Class	No	Name		Score	/10

Unit 20	Part 1	Part 2	Part 3	Part 4		
	1. Ⓐ Ⓑ Ⓒ Ⓓ	3. Ⓐ Ⓑ Ⓒ	7. Ⓐ Ⓑ Ⓒ Ⓓ	9. Ⓐ Ⓑ Ⓒ Ⓓ		
	2. Ⓐ Ⓑ Ⓒ Ⓓ	4. Ⓐ Ⓑ Ⓒ	8. Ⓐ Ⓑ Ⓒ Ⓓ	10. Ⓐ Ⓑ Ⓒ Ⓓ		
		5. Ⓐ Ⓑ Ⓒ				
		6. Ⓐ Ⓑ Ⓒ				
	Class	No	Name		Score	/10

Review Test 1	Part 1	Part 2	Part 3	Part 4		
	1. Ⓐ Ⓑ Ⓒ Ⓓ	5. Ⓐ Ⓑ Ⓒ	10. Ⓐ Ⓑ Ⓒ Ⓓ	13. Ⓐ Ⓑ Ⓒ Ⓓ		
	2. Ⓐ Ⓑ Ⓒ Ⓓ	6. Ⓐ Ⓑ Ⓒ	11. Ⓐ Ⓑ Ⓒ Ⓓ	14. Ⓐ Ⓑ Ⓒ Ⓓ		
	3. Ⓐ Ⓑ Ⓒ Ⓓ	7. Ⓐ Ⓑ Ⓒ	12. Ⓐ Ⓑ Ⓒ Ⓓ	15. Ⓐ Ⓑ Ⓒ Ⓓ		
	4. Ⓐ Ⓑ Ⓒ Ⓓ	8. Ⓐ Ⓑ Ⓒ				
		9. Ⓐ Ⓑ Ⓒ				
	Class	No	Name		Score	/15

Review Test 2	Part 1	Part 2	Part 3	Part 4		
	1. Ⓐ Ⓑ Ⓒ Ⓓ	5. Ⓐ Ⓑ Ⓒ	10. Ⓐ Ⓑ Ⓒ Ⓓ	13. Ⓐ Ⓑ Ⓒ Ⓓ		
	2. Ⓐ Ⓑ Ⓒ Ⓓ	6. Ⓐ Ⓑ Ⓒ	11. Ⓐ Ⓑ Ⓒ Ⓓ	14. Ⓐ Ⓑ Ⓒ Ⓓ		
	3. Ⓐ Ⓑ Ⓒ Ⓓ	7. Ⓐ Ⓑ Ⓒ	12. Ⓐ Ⓑ Ⓒ Ⓓ	15. Ⓐ Ⓑ Ⓒ Ⓓ		
	4. Ⓐ Ⓑ Ⓒ Ⓓ	8. Ⓐ Ⓑ Ⓒ				
		9. Ⓐ Ⓑ Ⓒ				
	Class	No	Name		Score	/15

Review Test 3	Part 1	Part 2	Part 3	Part 4		
	1. Ⓐ Ⓑ Ⓒ Ⓓ	5. Ⓐ Ⓑ Ⓒ	10. Ⓐ Ⓑ Ⓒ Ⓓ	13. Ⓐ Ⓑ Ⓒ Ⓓ		
	2. Ⓐ Ⓑ Ⓒ Ⓓ	6. Ⓐ Ⓑ Ⓒ	11. Ⓐ Ⓑ Ⓒ Ⓓ	14. Ⓐ Ⓑ Ⓒ Ⓓ		
	3. Ⓐ Ⓑ Ⓒ Ⓓ	7. Ⓐ Ⓑ Ⓒ	12. Ⓐ Ⓑ Ⓒ Ⓓ	15. Ⓐ Ⓑ Ⓒ Ⓓ		
	4. Ⓐ Ⓑ Ⓒ Ⓓ	8. Ⓐ Ⓑ Ⓒ				
		9. Ⓐ Ⓑ Ⓒ				
	Class	No	Name		Score	/15

Review Test 4	Part 1	Part 2	Part 3	Part 4		
	1. Ⓐ Ⓑ Ⓒ Ⓓ	5. Ⓐ Ⓑ Ⓒ	10. Ⓐ Ⓑ Ⓒ Ⓓ	13. Ⓐ Ⓑ Ⓒ Ⓓ		
	2. Ⓐ Ⓑ Ⓒ Ⓓ	6. Ⓐ Ⓑ Ⓒ	11. Ⓐ Ⓑ Ⓒ Ⓓ	14. Ⓐ Ⓑ Ⓒ Ⓓ		
	3. Ⓐ Ⓑ Ⓒ Ⓓ	7. Ⓐ Ⓑ Ⓒ	12. Ⓐ Ⓑ Ⓒ Ⓓ	15. Ⓐ Ⓑ Ⓒ Ⓓ		
	4. Ⓐ Ⓑ Ⓒ Ⓓ	8. Ⓐ Ⓑ Ⓒ				
		9. Ⓐ Ⓑ Ⓒ				
	Class	No	Name		Score	/15

〈キ リ ト リ 線〉